FROM STRESS TO SUCCESS

IN 5 EASY LESSONS!

DR. ROGER CAREY

In Memory of my Mother, Rosetta Mae Carey
(March 19, 2019)

"I Can Do All Things Through Christ Who Strengthens Me."

PHILIPPIANS 4:13

PREFACE

Most people are going about managing stress in the wrong ways. Empirical research into managing stress provides you with many interventions and uses, but lacks more emphasis on positive psychology, resilience, and our thinking processes. This book demonstrates 5 Easy Lessons to go from Stress to Success! The techniques provided here will enhance your development of necessary skills to combat stress and help you to reach an optimal conclusion.

This book is about what people can do for themselves right now in order to relieve chronic stress that may have caused you to feel less hopeful, and not very optimistic about yourself. The responsibility to take action relies on the individual. Taking action and following these guidelines will prove to be successful and help to motivate you into action steps and much Success.

Managing stress and utilizing techniques to alleviate the pressure and anxiety associated with chronic stress is used all over the world, in clinics, hospitals, institutions, as well as groups, classes, and churches, in order to help people to get the appropriate relief. There are many therapists, teachers, pastors, psychologists, and treatment centers that regularly recommend these interventions to patients, and thousands of readers, with the hope that individuals will gain the necessary skills needed to conquer stress in their lives and become much more at peace within themselves.

FOREWORD

BY KHULOUD D. ZEID

I am delighted to have the honor to write a brief foreword to this book, "Stress to Success in 5 Easy Lessons," written by Dr. Roger Carey.

Maintaining a balanced life, proactive with coping mechanisms, will help handle the surplus of stressors that inevitably emerge in our daily lives. Distress is a natural part of life; if stress left abandoned after some time can prompt burnouts with emotional fatigue, loss of one's compassion, mindfulness, and insight, and a diminished feeling of achievement. Experiencing stress is part of everyday life, regardless of working with troublesome challenges, adapting to work demands, family issues, financial concerns, and many other intense and unending difficulties and stressors in our lives. Whenever left untreated, compassion fatigue not exclusively can influence mental and physical well-being. Because life is a loop of ups and downs, and if we were to take it easy and work through it to move on to the better by developing the techniques/coping mechanism as a way to overcome stress.

Moreover, to focus on the next step of moving forward and not letting our negative thinking control our future of moving forward. This book answers the common inquiries, difficulties, and their management in an easy-to-understand manner. This book is comprehensive in all respects as a guide to stress management. The lucid language and delivery of illustrations make it easy for the readers to understand. The book is divided into step-by-step for the reader to learn the process of stress management, making it easy to immediately answer questions or concerns and help guide you to coping mechanisms/techniques to manage stress.

It is comprehensive, covering essential aspects of stress management in the easy five-step lesson to success and teaching coping strategies and alternative remedies to overcome stress. It will be a helpful guidebook to all, making it a pleasurable and informational learning experience for the reader. I wish Dr. Roger Carey all the very best and am confident that this book will greatly succeed.

KHULOUD D. ZEID

Arizona State University Graduate

Social Justice and Human Rights, MA

INTRODUCTION

What is Stress?

No matter how old you are, you will have stress in your life. Whether it is good stress, bad stress or too much stress, you cannot escape from it.

But what exactly is stress?

The official definition of stress is "a condition that occurs in response to actual or anticipated difficulties in life."

For some people, stress at home is making their life miserable, while other people find it extremely difficult to get through a stress-filled day on the job.

When stress starts to take over your life, it is time to take some drastic measures. You can learn how to manage your stress before it takes a toll on your health. If left untreated, stress can lead to a wide range of medical problems, including:

- High blood pressure
- Sleep disorders
- Back pain

- Heart disease
- Stroke
- Severe headaches

Stress can also lead to overeating or eating too much junk food, which eventually will raise your cholesterol level and put you in danger of having a heart attack or a stroke.

Sounds somewhat scary, doesn't it?

Well, it is. And if you are feeling stressed out, you are not alone. According to the United States National Institute for Occupational Safety and Health, stress related disorders are becoming the most prevalent reason for worker disability. Medical researchers estimate that over 200 million people take some type of medication every week for stress-related symptoms. This means that stress is no laughing matter!

Recognizing the Warning Signs of Stress

Stress can attack you on both a physical and psychological level. Learn to recognize the warning signs and you will be better off.

Psychological Signs of Stress

- A tendency to worry too much
- Having a short fuse that often leads to anger
- Experiencing mood swings and sudden bouts of sadness
- A loss of your sense of humor

Physical Signs of Stress

- Frequent occurrences of heartburn, indigestion and an upset stomach

- Difficulty sleeping at night
- A throat as dry as the Sahara Desert
- The urge to overeat
- A loss of appetite
- Increased muscle tension

If you are suffering from too much stress in your life, there is hope. Keep reading and you will discover some creative ways to deal with any stress that comes your way!

1

LESSON NUMBER ONE

Understand Resilience and Stress

Resilience is the ability to adapt well when confronted with adversity, trauma, and inordinate levels of stress in life. One needs to exercise flexibility, in that strengths and resources usually held in reserve may be tapped under circumstances requiring extraordinary effort or unusual challenges.

The following are changes we hope to see in the change process:

- New perceptions of oneself (feeling stronger, more self-assured)
- Gains in recognizing and appreciating one's vulnerability
- Change in relationship with others (closer family ties and more appreciation of significant others)
- Changed philosophy of life (taking things easier, greater spirituality

In these next few pages, we will address some common questions that people have about stress...

Is it really possible to overcome stress in order to become successful?

Research tells us that stress can be a motivator to help us be invigorated to pursue our goals and objectives. With just enough stress to get us going, to activate our norephedrine, the biological neurochemicals in the brain, we can ultimately achieve anything we pursue. Stress moves us, motivates us and activates brain chemistry to get us moving. It puts us under enough pressure to move forward, progress, and sprint ahead on our journey through life. It serves as a mechanism for strength, power, energy, and desire to reach toward the sky and go after our goals/dreams.

In my private practice in psychology and my ministry, I have taught thousands of people over decades to utilize the power of positive thinking, to believe in themselves, and to PRACTICE these principles daily.

Overcoming stress not only takes practice, but one needs to develop positive coping mechanisms. Developing coping strategies will miraculously change the situation, the tension, the worry, the anxiety, and the belief behind all of these things. Moreover, learning to activate distress tolerance techniques will quell the stress. It will help the individual to handle problems and situations much more successfully.

How much is "stress and motivation" related? Are they always good? Or bad? Or in-between? How can people "harness" their motivation for good, and not fall prey to the stress that might come with it?

According to research studies, findings suggest that stress can serve as a motivator to get people into action. To take action, to move their lives forward. If we didn't have stress as a motivator, many people would not have become as successful as they are in their careers, relationships, and pursuit of happiness! Stress takes us where we need to go, good or bad. Learning to utilize the stress factor will pay off dividends to our lives.

There are two types of personalities. One, where the individual views everything as a stress or challenge, and the other where one sees the good in everything. They meet the challenges head-on with enthusiasm. To decrease the stress in our lives means we must change the way we think and the way we view the world, and our perspectives on how we see/view what happens to us, good or bad. It is not the stress that will ultimately bring us down, it's how we see it, and what good can come of it. *We* are the captains of our ship. *We* decide how we will approach stress in our live.

To conquer stress, there's a need for transformation. We must overhaul our lives. We must change the way we think, and change our brains wiring. Our brains are like computers; we have to change the hardware, the software and continue with updates. As we change our thoughts, thus, we change our lives. It really is that simple!

Can you explain in "simple terms" what the "cause and effects" of stress are?

From a biological standpoint, stress is caused by neurological mis-firings in the brain. The brain is overwhelmed with too much stimuli, and too many active neurons. Additionally, its multi-causal, multiple factors intersecting at once. The evidence suggests that much of our stress is centered in genes. Much of it comes from our parents. In childhood, where it all began, if you were deemed a difficult child to raise, it is most likely you were given too much anxiety, and were not equipped to handle things very well. Your stress levels were much more intense than the child that was an easy baby to raise, without too much stress involved.

People almost never view stress as a "positive" event. How can they better understand that concept?

Stress as a positive event that can indeed be our teacher, guide, and mentor regarding life's challenges, and unknowns. If it were not for stress, we would be less inclined to be motivated, successful, active, and interested in life and all the wonders the world has to offer. Stress does not have to restrict us, limit us, or bound us up to where we become debilitated. It serves a different purpose. It makes up much more alert, cognizant that we need to act, to get into motion, to respond to life's challenges. Stress does not have to cause physical, emotional, or psychological strain. From a psychological perspective, we can view stress as our body's response to anything that requires attention or action. Everyone experiences stress to some degree. The way in which you respond to the stressors will make a big difference to your overall well-being and happiness.

Why does stress "get us going" and (hopefully) gives us a strong desire to achieve?

The benefits of stress are that it gets us going. If we don't activate our system through stress, then we fall short of actively pursuing our goals and objectives. Researchers have studied the Cortisol Awakening Response (CAR) and have found that cortisol is the highest in individuals who lead high stress lives. This is a biological determinant. We can overcome genes, through practice and acknowledgment that we have these high levels and we need to work to bring our levels of stress to the normal range. At the same time, we need just enough stress to assist us with achieving our potential and reaching our goals in life.

As human beings, we are very similar to each other. We have the same responses, challenges, thoughts, and sometimes beliefs about what it means to be successful. Stress will help that process if we understand it better and the purpose that it serves.

"Stress and Strength." Really? If it's true, why? But don't most people see them as exact opposites?

Science tells us that the more attention we pay to our strengths, the less we will be concerned about our stressful lives. Too much stress leads to poor quality, or state of being physically strong. Some may view it as weakness, a sense of powerlessness, and ultimately debilitation. One might view stress as showing resistance to the external load. Strength on the other hand, demonstrates a tolerance for the material at hand and its property. In my private practice and ministry, I have taught individuals how to focus on character strengths as positive personality traits.   What I discovered through many years of practice and results from patients, character strengths correlate with good coping strategies, and often serve as a buffer to stress and overall satisfaction. Many research studies have examined these phenomena and concluded that character strengths are trainable personal characteristics that improve coping, and decreases the negative effects of stress.

How I can adjust and adapt to stressful times!

Research studies have found significant correlations between stress and ways to adapt to stress. One needs to find humor in the situation. Psychotherapy, priests, pastors, and the like are coping strategies that can be utilized and produce good outcomes. For decades people have found that talking about our stressors relieves or reduces the amount of stress on our brains and bodies. I have taught individuals how to not stress about stressing out. To focus on their values instead of their fears, for example. To accept the past, and fight like hell for the future. Never expect stability. Life doesn't work that way. We are students in life. We are here to learn from our errors and not repeat them. Stress is our teacher. We can learn to overcome the tension, worry, strain, fears, and trauma from our pasts.

To cope better in stressful times, set aside leisure times. Do something you enjoy every day. By all means, keep your sense of humor! Start a practice of meditation, relaxation techniques, and exercise with good sleep practices. Never over-commit yourselves. As much as you can, prioritize your tasks, and break projects into small steps.

How can someone better manage their stress to achieve more favorable outcomes?

We all want to be successful in life. I think most of us were not prepared for life from the beginning. Maybe it was bad parenting, addictions, dysfunctional families, not raised right, not given a set of instructions on life and how to be successful. Whatever the case may be, none of us have received proper training to meet life on life's terms. I teach my patients to give their minds a rest. To acknowledge that we may have to reprogram our brains, reparent ourselves, to rehabilitate from all the errors we've made and to start fresh with new ideas, better science, greater knowledge, and attend workshops, webinars, college classes, and other support systems to combat stress. Take time to rebalance our lives, work, home, relationships. To build a structure around regular exercise, proper nutrition/diet, connection with supportive people, positive thinking,

Stress Busting Tips:

1. **Get a good night's sleep.** How much sleep did you get last night? Was it enough for you? Most people do not get enough sleep, and that can cause you to begin your workday already feeling stressed. Stop falling asleep on the sofa and go to bed. Set a goal of trying to get at least 7 to 8 hours of sleep each night. Give your body a chance to relax and you will wake up refreshed and ready to begin your day.

2. **Eat your breakfast.** Before you shout, "Breakfast, who has time for breakfast?" remember that we all have the same amount of time: 24 hours

a day. Set your alarm clock twenty minutes earlier and eat something nutritious before you head out to work. Even if you only have a piece of toast, a glass of orange juice and some fruit, at least you are getting something nourishing into your body.

3. **Get some exercise.** If you can rearrange your schedule to make time for breakfast, you can do the same to include exercise. Exercise can do wonders to relieve the stress in your body and in your mind. Take a few moments and do several jumping jacks and arm and leg stretches. Walk or jog in place, and before you know it you will begin to feel better.

2

LESSON NUMBER TWO

Take A Proactive Approach to Stress Management and Prevention

Abraham Maslow was among the first theorists to explore what is right with people instead of what is wrong with them. As most individuals know from first-hand-experience, much of psychology is devoted to labeling human experience in terms of problems. Maslow, however, was curious about what we could learn from those individuals who are at the top of the mental health scale instead of those who are struggling at the bottom.

- Focus on positive experiences, positive character traits
- Focus on human strengths such as courage, optimism, and hope that can serve as buffers against stress-related problems
- Self-Acceptance—Develop high regard for yourself —as a person, in spite of one's limitations, mistakes and failures. Honest assessment of

strengths and weaknesses. Develop compassion
and understanding not only for others but also for
yourself

In these next few pages, we will address some additional
questions that people have about stress...

How does stress lead to unwanted addictions, including alcohol and drug abuse/dependence?

Research suggests that when an individual experiences too much stress in their lives it can potentially lead to an increasing amount of drug and alcohol abuse. There are high incidences where people, both men and women, rely on drug use and alcohol as a form of coping strategy. Moreover, it may be used as a form of escape from their current reality. With consistent use and abuse of these drugs, people eventually form a habit to these substances and become addicted to street drugs and alcohol as they use them quite often as their choice of medication to offset any disturbances occurring in their brains and with their ability to function appropriately in their daily living.

Our society is encountering a huge epidemic that appears to be out of proportion with substance use and dependence on chemicals to combat unwanted stress in their lives. Science tells us that substance use and dependence is a learned behavior. Like any other addiction, learned behavior is created from continuous maladaptive behavior through repetition, and their brains telling them that they have to have it in order to cope well, function well, and adapt to their various stressors in their lives.

Is it really true that stress can affect our immune system?

Scientists have done considerable amounts of research on the effects that chronic stress has on our immune system. Current research indicates that when we are stressed, the immune system's ability to fight off antigens is reduced. This may be why we tend to be more susceptible to infections. According to a report published by the American Psychological Association, long-term, chronic stress weakens the responses to your immune system. If you repeatedly feel anxious and stressed or it lasts a long time, your body never gets the signal to return to normal functioning. This can potentially lead to a weakened immune system, that ultimately will leave you more vulnerable to viral infections and more frequent illnesses.

To combat the negative effects to our immune system from too much stress in our lives, one needs to take a hard look at how and why stress will eventually compromise our ability to function well and avoid these pitfalls. Let's suppose physical symptoms may cause or make your mental state; it's called psychosomatic. Moreover, most people in our society believe that psychosomatic symptoms aren't real. That is, they believe they are made up. Not so. In current research studies it has been demonstrated in fact, very real symptoms that have a psychological cause.

One needs to pay closer attention to their mental health. Strengthening our mental health can lessen the effects of symptoms on our immune system. At times when you feel troubled, it is time to get active and keep active. Keep in touch with others who have your best interest in mind. Ask for help. Do something that you are good at. We want to discourage high stress levels that can cause depression and anxiety symptoms to exaggerate, leading to higher levels of inflammation, which leads to an over-tired immune system that can't properly protect you.

Why can't we "just be stressed?" Does stress really lead to strokes, heart disease and overall poor health?

Our society has been discussing the effects of stress on the body/mind/spirit connection for decades. How often have your family members, friends and associates shared stories of their loved ones becoming impaired, debilitated, compromised, or have an even shorter lifespan due to the stress factor? Of paramount interest, people want to know if stress can actually lead to strokes, heart disease, and overall poor health. The answer to these questions has remained the same for decades. Doctors and medical clinics, psychologists, and other professionals in the helping fields have supported the body of research which have warned us for decades to keep our stress levels to a minimum. Parents, teachers, spouses, medical professions have given us a boatload of information on how to take care of ourselves in relation to ward off the negative effects of stress and live more healthily.

In my interviews with many of my patients over the span of 35-years, as I conduct a medical history along with a psychological history, many patients have been concerned about having too much stress and often ask, "can stress permanently damage my heart?" I always tell them they need to be in control of their stress, anxiety, and depression. Having too much stress, for too long, *IS* bad for your heart. If you have high levels of stress in your life, you must find good ways to manage it, or you will likely have heart disease, high blood pressure, chest pain, or irregular heartbeats.

Stress Busting Tips:

1. **Get the right attitude.** Do you know that your attitude is your most prized possession? It is something that you and only you own and control. No one can take it away from you, so it is important to begin each day with the right attitude. By having a positive attitude, you set the tone for your whole day.

2. **Stop worrying.** When you find yourself worrying too much, stress will find a way in. Sometimes it helps to simply make a list of what is worrying you and then look for creative solutions for each problem. While no one can live completely worry-free, you can reduce the amount of time you spend worrying.

3. **Avoid stressful commutes.** For example, try using a road that has less traffic, and you won't get caught up in everyone else's road rage problems. If someone wants to pass you, let them. Take a few seconds when the light changes before proceeding. And make sure you allow plenty of time to travel to your job. You can cause your own stress attack by leaving late and then worrying about how you can get to your job on time.

3

LESSON NUMBER THREE

Understand Your Emotional Intelligence (EI)

The concept of emotional intelligence has broadened the notion of IQ and capitalized different strengths to combat stress. Consider these:

- **Self-Awareness**: identify and recognize your emotions as they are occurring. This also includes being aware of the relationship between thoughts, feelings and actions
- **Expressing Feelings**: This includes the skills of accurately and effectively communicating feelings in ways that are likely to be heard and understood.
- **Reading Others**: empathy involves the ability to walk in other people's shoes and know what they must be feeling. This allows one to look at things from multiple perspectives, and to feel compassion for others
- **Motivating Action**: it is not enough to become aware of feelings in yourself or others; you must be

willing to respond appropriately based on this knowledge

- **Managing Relationships**: this involves responding effectively to feelings when they arise and resolving interpersonal conflicts

In these next few pages, we will address still more additional questions that people have about stress...

What are some "easy to learn" stress management techniques? And do some work better than others?

The science literature examines stress reduction techniques and boils it down to the following easy to learn techniques to combat stress in individuals lives. The first, and probably the most effective strategy that we could employ is **adequate exercise regimen.** Working out regularly and being consistent with this practice will pay dividends to our health and emotional well-being; and this is one of the best ways to relax your brain and your body.

Take note: One absolutely should focus on muscle groups of the body, meaning relax your muscles. This is referred to as **Progressive Muscle Relaxation.** When you are stressed, your muscles get tense. Put simply, start this practice by tightening up your muscles from your head to your toes. Tighten every muscle as hard as you can, then release, and go through, step-by-step with each of your muscle groups.

Deep breathing. Most people you ask about this technique will say they believe it works. Problem is, they don't engage in this unique practice enough. Carve out a special time of the today to simply take deep breaths, exhaling, and inhaling, slowly, and persistently.

Slow down. Most of us lead busy lives. We are racing

against the clock to be as productive as we can. To reach our high expectations, and to please our bosses, and spouses. And we often forget that our bodies are not designed to constantly be racing full speed ahead, while leaving our bodies and minds behind. Slowing down means taking the time to notice our surroundings, to pay more attention to the ones we love most, to capture the moment so that we don't miss out on the beauty of the earth that surrounds us at any given time. Maybe we might try some guided imagery. Guided imagery is like taking a short vacation in your mind.

Expand your stress management toolkit by mastering healthy, positive coping mechanisms. Be mindful of what you eat and drink. Get enough sleep. The mind and the body require adequate rest and relaxation so that the brain can function optimally.

How important is prayer and meditation when it comes to learning how to manage our stress? Does it work for everyone? Including children?

Prayer and meditation are an ancient practice that's been around for centuries for the relief of, and management of stress. How can prayer and meditation make you healthier and stronger in the fight against the negative effects of stress? They can assist you with an improved sense of well-being, lowering stress in the body, lower blood pressure, lower frequency of hospitalizations, and increase one's longevity. How do we utilize meditation? We can start by practicing focused concentration, bringing yourself back to the moment over and over again, which actually addresses stress, whether positive or negative. Meditation also reduces areas of anxiety, chronic pain, depression, heart disease and high blood pressure.

There are many positive benefits of a spiritual practice.

With the understanding that spirituality is different for everyone, many people have found that having a spiritual or religious practice helps with stress management. For example, a spiritual side can offer an individual a boost by allowing God or a higher power and surrendering worries and troubles, rather than holding on so tightly to stress.

The benefits of science-based meditation are controlling anxiety, promoting emotional health, enhancing awareness, reducing age-related memory loss, generating more kindness and compassion, and fighting off addictions.

Is it true that getting enough exercise, enough sleep and maintaining positive, social relationships will help us to manage our stress?

Recent research suggests getting enough sleep, regular exercise and maintaining positive, healthy relationships, can, indeed, reduce one's stress profoundly. Moreover, it can have a profound effect on depression and anxiety. Let's begin by dissecting the concept of exercise/physical activity. Research all along has been telling us that exercise and other physical activity produces endorphins, oxytocin, and other chemicals in the brain that act as natural painkillers. Additionally, they participate to improve one's ability to sleep, which is a good vehicle to reduce stress. It has been often said that sleep is a powerful stress reducer. Following a regular sleep pattern calms and restores the body and the brain. Moreover, it improves concentration, regulates mood symptoms, and sharpens judgment and decision-making.

Aerobic exercise is key for your brain, just as it is for your heart. Most people will likely not agree at first; indeed, the first steps are the hardest, and in the beginning, exercise will be more work than fun. When people begin to get into shape, they will begin to tolerate exercise, and enjoy it, and even depend on it. Behavioral factors also contribute to the emotional benefits of exercise. You begin to have more strength and stamina. You earn a sense of mastery and control, of pride and self-confidence.

The old adage, you can lead a horse to water, but you can't make it drink, holds true, even for humans. Why do human beings resist change? What are the potential barriers to change? What are their fears, insecurities, and how does that stop them from progressing? I think daily stress can have a major impact on one's mental and physical health. Managing stress requires work, effort, being consistent, and driven to succeed. One needs to identify the causes of stress, and recognize the signs of stress.

Oftentimes, resistance to change may stem from lack of awareness of why change is needed, and how it would impact them positively. It's funny, people likely will not change if they don't have solid reasons to change or don't understand the consequences of not changing. Perhaps people resist change because they think it's going to bring about something different, something unexpected. Moreover, they may fear not knowing what the outcome could bring. What about this: Are people afraid they will lose something of value? Or fear they will not be able to adapt to the new ways? Maybe it's deeply emotional because of their level of safety and security.

Positive attitudes and positive activities...are they related? If so, how? And how important are they in the "stress tool box?"

There is power in positive thinking. Positive psychology is a school of thought that centers on the characteristics of optimism, positive thinking, the benefits of happiness, healthy relationships, and other constructs that help an individual attain optimal functioning. This theory purports that positive thinking helps with stress management and can, indeed, promote health and better well-being. Therefore, positive thinking is key to effective stress management. When one engages in the power of positive thinking, one will immediately see a reduction in their stress levels, and will help with the individual feeling better about themselves. Their outlook on life will change significantly.

It's been proven by research studies that when an individual is stressed out, they consequently have a poor attitude on top of that stress, which can spike your stress levels until it's off the charts. I think the majority of people would benefit greatly from looking at adversity straight in the eye, and meet those challenges head-on. Learn that you get what you get in life, and don't pitch a fit about it. Be accepting, flexible, open-minded, and improve your tolerance for challenges that come our way unexpectedly. Focus on enjoying the unexpected, even if it's not what you wanted originally.

Stress Busting Tips:

1. **Set goals for yourself**. Know what you need to accomplish each day on your job. If you have a very stressful job, make a list of the things you need to work on, and concentrate on them one at a time. When you become organized and have goals in your work life, stress can be kept at bay.

2. **Slow down.** Research has proven that when someone slows down, they actually accomplish more than people who are rushing around. Concentrate on the tasks at hand and focus on what it is you are trying to accomplish. When you slow down, your concentration increases, and you work smarter, not harder.

3. **Improve your time management skills.**
   Everyone has 24 hours a day, 7 days a week. When
   you choose to spend your time wisely, you feel
   good about yourself and everything you have
   accomplished. Read a book on time management,
   attend a workshop or simply sit down and
   brainstorm creative ways you can improve your use
   of time.

4

LESSON NUMBER FOUR

Move Toward Your Peak Performance: From Stress to Success

We are constantly being evaluated, or evaluating ourselves. A lot of research has been completed on peak performance. Peak performance can be measured in terms of how a person's behavior stands out against others, but it can also be assessed according to how well it compares with that person's unique potential.

Here are some tips that will help you go from Stress to Success:

- Maintain contact with your extended family
- Engage in spiritual practices
- Maintain good health
- Live in a stimulating environment, based on your values
- Work toward a coherent set of goals
- Rest, relax, and take holidays in moderation
- Make leisure activities a priority

- Avoid distressing situation when possible
- Focus on the positive as much as you can
- Keep an optimistic upbeat attitude in which you expect success
- Challenge perfectionistic thinking and unrealistic expectations
- Dispute irrational thoughts that lead to upsetting feelings

In these next few pages, we will address some additional questions that people have about stress...

Why is stress so overwhelming to some people that they can't understand the need to seek professional help?

Understanding stress and how it affects us is vitally important. When people are overwhelmed, they are often beset with intense emotion that can be difficult to manage. Most often, it affects one's ability to think and act rationally. Emotional overwhelm is caused by chronic stress, traumatic life experiences, relationship issues and much more.

Feelings of unpredictability and complete despair can fuel feelings of being overwhelmed, and cause a person to experience significant distress. When one arrives in an emotional state of mind wherein you have reached total overwhelm, you will likely not seek professional help. Here's why: you may be experiencing low energy, headaches, upset stomach, aches, pains, chest pain, insomnia, and frequent colds and depression and anxiety symptoms. When we find ourselves in this state of mind, it's very difficult to reach out and ask for the help that we need.

Why should people seek professional help for stress,

chronic distress, and feelings that are so overwhelming that they find themselves in a dysfunctional state of mental health? Why don't individuals seek out help for managing stress? These are just a few of the question's psychologists have sought to answer over many decades.

If we decide not to seek help for managing our extreme stress levels, this may seriously lead to anxiety and depression. If your depressed mood lasts for more than two weeks, or is seriously interfering with your ability to function at work, with your family, or in your social life, it would be a very good idea that you consult with a professional. Chronic stress disrupts nearly every system in your body. Moreover, should you ignore these symptoms, it can suppress your immune system, upset your digestive system, and reproductive systems, increase the risk of heart attack and stroke, and most likely speed up the aging process.

Is it true that socialization is important to a well-balanced and complete life?

It is important to understand that socialization is part of life-span development. This process continues throughout an individual's life. In the scientific literature, it is purported that sociologists believe socialization is a lifelong process of inheriting and disseminating norms, customs and ideologies, providing an individual with the skills and habits necessary for participating within his or her own society.

Socialization is not the same as socializing. Socializing is to mix with others socially, i.e., friends, family, neighbors, co-workers, whereas socialization is a process that may include *socializing* as one element, but it is a more complex, multi-faceted and a formative set of interactive experiences. Moreover, it is also an adaptive, lifelong experience, because society is constantly changing, and we often find ourselves in new situations.

Socialization is critical both to individuals and the societies in which they live. As individuals, social interaction provides us the means by which we gradually become able to see ourselves through the eyes of others, and how we learn who we are, and how we fit into the larger world. Additionally, to function successfully in society, we have to learn the basics of how to strike a balance in our lives so that we don't become so distressed by our environment, our work, our families, and our day-to-day activities.

For society to function, the socialization of individuals is necessary. Without socialization, we would not have a society or culture. And without social interaction, we would not have socialization. Socialization prepares people to participate in a social group by teaching them its norms and expectations.

In order for individuals to have a complete and well-balanced life, some of the benefits of socialization may be found in having confidence, good self-esteem, and increased quality of life, reduced blood pressure, and a boost in immunity and other physical health benefits. Having a balance in life promotes purpose and increased brain health.

To function well in our society, we need interaction with friends and family. The ancient philosopher, Aristotle once said, "We are Social Animals." In other words, we quite frankly are highly dependent upon others for our strength, wisdom, knowledge, prosperity, and overall success in life. Our society is one of the most important parts of our lives.

One might ponder the question, what is a well-balanced life? And how might we obtain that standard? Many scientific studies have purported that living a well- balanced life means determining what is important to you and expanding your time and attention to these ideals accordingly. To achieve this, one needs to put energy into not being so busy, or overcommitted. Finding peace and solace should be celebrated and encouraged.

Having a balanced lifestyle means incorporation of a positive/optimistic outlook, focusing on positive, sound, good habits, and doing everything possible to lower our stress levels. We all long to live healthy and happy lifestyles. Balanced living means protecting ourselves from poor mental and emotional health, too.

A balanced life may include having clear priorities, knowing when we should say no to responsibilities/obligations that we just don't have time to attend to. Being proactive in managing our energies, exercising, and looking for enjoyable activities every day. Research tells us that being well-balanced would essentially mean that we are sensible, that we do not have many emotional problems...that we are fun loving, rational, level headed, and well adjusted.

Why is it important to find/create/have a spiritual life?

For centuries people have asked why is it important to have or create a spiritual life? Moreover, people have been pondering the questions of what is the purpose of life, why am I here, what happens to individuals after they die? Theologians, psychologists, and philosophers have researched these and many other questions related to the significance of having a spiritual life and the benefits from achieving these ideals. From the volumes of research on this matter, one can conclude, A spiritually healthy individual has a clear purpose in life and is able to reflect on the meaning of events. In addition, these individuals have clearly defined ideas of right and wrong and are able to act accordingly. I think being spiritual most clearly means pursuing a general sense of harmony and self-awareness. Moreover, attaining a sense of peace, wholeness, and balance among the physical, emotional, social and spiritual aspects of our life.

Your spiritual life determines your character, your perspective, and the way in which you relate to the world around you. It's essentially about self-care, and being our best. Having developed a spiritual life may also mean helping us to better deal with the world, people around us, situations that may seem overwhelming and challenging, and to grow into a better, more whole and healthier person. Thus, it enables us to handle and manage our stress far better than ever before.

Stress Busting Tips:

1. **Laugh out loud.** When was the last time you laughed out loud? You have probably heard the saying "laughter is the best medicine," and it is true. Get in touch with your inner sense of humor, and watch your stress evaporate. Start by reading the comics in the daily newspaper, or listening to your favorite comedian on a CD. There are thousands of websites that have jokes and funny stories. Visit a few today and start laughing out loud.

2. **Listen to raindrops.** The next time it is raining when you are at home, take a few minutes and listen to the raindrops. There is something very peaceful about rain, and listening to the raindrops will help alleviate any stress you are experiencing. Alternatively, buy a CD of sounds of a rain shower.

3. **Pet your dog.** Or cat, or whatever pet you happen to have at home. Medical research has proven that your blood pressure drops when you

begin to pet an animal. Although your day at home might be so hectic you wish you lived on another planet, try petting the dog and let it snuggle with you. You'll be amazed at how you will begin to feel better in just a few moments.

5

LESSON NUMBER FIVE

Learn Positive Stress Management and
Prevention Techniques

Based on recent research on positive psychology, optimal functioning, and making changes last, one might feel intrigued enough to want to apply these lessons and concepts to enhance one's strengths. Think about stress in terms not only of its presence but also of its absence. Focus on the times when you demonstrate tranquility and control.

To offset the debilitating effects of stress:

- Accept the fact that stress is an inevitable part of life and decide to respond to it positively
- Prevent stress by studying your usual patterns of vulnerability—look at the stressor, and your perception to that distress and response, and subsequent consequences
- Find out what you love to do and plunge into it—it is a matter of finding a calling, something that

speaks to you in such a way that you totally immerse yourself in the activity
- Turn stress into energy for success—initial negative energy can provide opportunities for constructive action
- Become more mindful about ways you can enjoy the present instead of ruminating about the past or worrying about the future
- Remember to breathe
- Stretch your body
- Take a break from technology
- Do one thing at a time
- Give or ask for a hug

In these next few pages, we will address some additional questions that people have about stress...

What is all of the fuss about the "neuroscience on stress and learning?" Is it important? Why?

Psychology and neuroscience have been researching the effects of stress and learning for decades. Recent research indicates Studies suggest that learning during or immediately after stress is often enhanced, stress disrupts memory retrieval and updating, and these effects are most pronounced for emotionally arousing material. Stress can affect how memories are formed. When stressed, people have a more difficult time creating short-term memories and turning those short-term memories into long-term memories, which means it's more difficult to learn when stressed.

Stress has mostly negative impacts on learning and

memory. However, a small amount of stress, particularly emotional (rather than physical) stress, during the encoding phase of memory can help a person retain new information.

What are some "instant" coping strategies for stress?

Strategies for coping with stress are abundant in the psychology literature.

Here are some highly effective coping strategies:

- Journaling about your emotions
- Using visualization strategies to increase positive feelings
- Using conflict resolution strategies to mitigate the stress in a relationship
- Release pent-up emotions
- Managing hostile feelings
- Mindfulness practices
- Limit information intake
- Keep a schedule and stay busy
- Read a book. Many public libraries have free digital downloads to a phone, tablet, or e-reader

What effects do stress have on my brain?

The effects to the brain from chronic stress and how this impacts the brain are topics of discussion among psychologists and neurologists. Interestingly enough, these effects include: stress can kill brain cells, and even reduce the size of the brain. Chronic stress has the effect of shrinking the brain at the prefrontal cortex, the area of the brain that's responsible for memory and learning.

"Your brain isn't just a single unit, but a group of different parts that performs different tasks," says Dr. Kerry, chief scientific officer at McLean, Hospital and professor of psychiatry at Harvard Medical School. Ressler. Stress affects not only memory and many other brain functions, like mood and anxiety, but also promotes inflammation, which adversely affects heart health.

Stress Busting Tips:

1. **Sleep in.** When is the last time you took time for yourself in the morning? There is no better way to beat stress at home than to spend a little extra time in bed. Too often people rush through life, running from one appointment to another, and the result is stress. Stop the stress now and then by taking time to sleep in.

2. **Spend a few minutes on the back porch.** When you are completely stressed out at home, spend a few minutes on the back porch or deck. (If you don't have either one, find a quiet place in the backyard.) Sit down and do nothing. Take a deep breath, and appreciate the fresh air and the solitude. Look up at the sky, and enjoy nature at its finest.

3. **Walk barefoot on the beach**. If you are fortunate enough to live near the beach, make sure you find time to walk barefoot. Just walk, and listen to the waves crashing against the shore. Feel the warm sand on your feet and toes. Your breathing will be more relaxed, and any stress you have been experiencing will soon disappear. If you live too far from the beach to take a walk, visualize

yourself there. Or listen to a CD with sounds of rhythmic waves at the beach as you visualize yourself being there. When you can begin using visualization techniques, you can beat stress no matter where you live.

ABOUT THE AUTHOR

DR. ROGER CAREY is a Licensed Clinical Psychologist who has extensive experience in stress management and prevention. Until recently, he had been working for the California Department of Corrections and Rehabilitation (CDCR), in addition to having his own thriving practice in Tracy, CA. Dr. Carey has treated patients with a variety of mental illnesses, including Bipolar Disorders, Schizophrenia, Addictions, Depression, PTSD and more. With his work over the past few decades, he has seen too many people fall victim to the "stress monster," and he has created a series of techniques to help alleviate the pressure and anxiety associated with stress. For more information, please visit www.drrogercarey.com.